MOVING
IN
GLORY
REALMS

STUDY GUIDE

MOVING IN GLORY REALMS

EXPLORING DIMENSIONS OF DIVINE PRESENCE

JOSHUA MILLS

WHITAKER
HOUSE

Unless otherwise indicated, all Scripture quotations are taken from the *Holy Bible, New International Version*®, NIV®, © 1973, 1978, 1984, 2011 by Biblica, Inc.® Used by permission. All rights reserved worldwide. The "NIV" and "New International Version" are trademarks registered in the United States Patent and Trademark Office by Biblica, Inc.®. Scripture quotation marked (BLB) is taken from *The Holy Bible, Berean Study Bible*, BSB, copyright © 2016 by Bible Hub. Used by Permission. All Rights Reserved Worldwide. Scripture quotations marked (NKJV) are taken from the *New King James Version*, © 1979, 1980, 1982 by Thomas Nelson, Inc. Used by permission. All rights reserved. Scripture quotations marked (NIV) are taken from Scripture quotations marked (AMP) are taken from *The Amplified® Bible*, © 2015 by The Lockman Foundation, La Habra, CA. Used by permission. (www.Lockman.org). All rights reserved.

Dictionary definitions are taken from Dictionary.com, unabridged, Random House, Inc.
Greek and Hebrew word definitions are taken from *Strong's Exhaustive Concordance of the Bible*.
Boldface type in the Scripture quotations indicates the author's emphasis.

Moving in Glory Realms Study Guide:
Exploring Dimensions of Divine Presence

International Glory Ministries
P.O. Box 4037
Palm Springs, CA 92263
JoshuaMills.com
info@joshuamills.com

ISBN: 978-1-64123-547-1
eBook ISBN: 978-1-64123-553-2
Printed in the United States of America
© 2020 by Joshua Mills

Whitaker House
1030 Hunt Valley Circle
New Kensington, PA 15068
www.whitakerhouse.com

1 2 3 4 5 6 7 8 9 10 11 ⨇ 27 26 25 24 23 22 21 20

CONTENTS

PART I: MOVING IN THE SPIRIT

1. Realms of Faith 9

2. Realms of Anointing 19

3. Realms of Glory 25

PART II: MOVING IN THE SUPERNATURAL

4. Realms of Divine Ascension 37

5. Realms of Angelic Presence 47

6. Realms of the Miraculous 55

PART III: MOVING IN THE HEAVENLIES

7. Realms of Manifesting Wealth 65

8. Realms of Spirit Travel 71

9. Realms of Heavenly Encounter 77

Study Guide Answers 87

About the Author 109

PART I

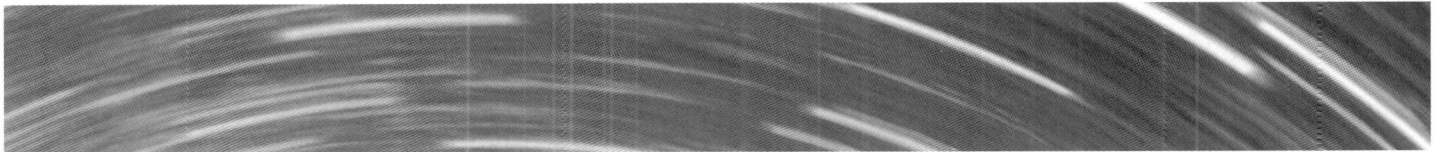

MOVING IN THE SPIRIT

REALMS OF FAITH

1. Everybody has faith! What does Romans 12:3 say?:

   _____

   _____

   _____

   _____

2. What kind of faith is pleasing to God?

   _____

3. When God wants to take us into a higher dimension of supernatural living, He invites us into a place of being _____.

4. Have you ever felt stretched in your faith? Explain your experience (use an additional sheet of paper if necessary):

_____

_____

_____

_____

_____

_____

_____

5. Faith gives birth to greater _____.

6. In Matthew 17:20, when it speaks about our faith being likened to a mustard seed, what does it mean? What are some specific qualities of the mustard seed?

_____

_____

_____

_____

_____

7. Our faith walk is a journey into securing our heavenly _____.

WE MUST BEGIN WITH FAITH

8. Faith is the starting point for all _____ _____.

For it is by grace you have been saved, through faith—and this is not from yourselves, it is the gift of God—not by works, so that no one can boast.

(Ephesians 2:8–9)

According to this verse, faith appropriates for us whatever is available by grace. Faith always releases the power for victory. (See 1 John 5:4.) Faith is miraculous and powerful. (See Romans 4:16–25.) Faith works by love. (See Galatians 5:6.)

9. Hebrews 11:1 says that "*faith is* _____ *in what we hope for and* _____ *about what we do not see.*"

10. Every realm in the Spirit is established and functions on the _____ of faith.

11. List three specific ways that you can build a solid foundation of faith, for your spiritual growth:

   1. _____

   2. _____

   3. _____

12. The basis for our sacred pilgrimage must be the _____ of who God is and what He does, and that requires _____.

THE IDENTITY OF FAITH

13. According to the dictionary, *faith is* "_____ _____ and _____ ____ and _____ to God," including "_____ _____ in something for which there is no proof."

14. Faith is the supernatural bridge between the _____ and the _____ _____. It is the spiritual force that pulls the future _____ of God into our here-and-now reality.

15. Faith grabs hold of the covenant promises of God and _____ them in the now.

16. We have this habit of putting the best things of God into the _____.

NEW SPIRITUAL FOUNDATIONS

17. You cannot put the new move of God into old traditions, habits, religious rites, ideas, or

    _____.

18. You cannot put _____ _____ with _____ _____

    because it spoils the freshness of it.

19. We utilize the substance of our faith to produce the _____ for it.

THE THREE DIMENSIONS OF FAITH

20. Name the three dimensions of faith and give a brief description of each.

    1. _____

    2. _____

    3. _____

21. What did the centurion of Matthew 8 have in common with the woman with the issue of blood
    from Matthew 9? _____ _____

22. Faith _____ God believes the miraculous is accessible when and how God permits. But the faith
    _____ God understands the New Covenant by divine revelation and knows that the miracle is
    available _____.

23. *"I have been _____ with Christ, and I no longer live, but Christ lives in me. And that
    which I now live in the flesh, I live through _____ from the Son of God, the One having loved me
    and having given up Himself for me."* (Galatians 2:20 BLB)

HAVING EARS TO HEAR

24. What is the meaning of the Greek word *logos*?

    _____

    _____

25. When your ears are open to hear God's _____ ____ _____, an infusion of God's mind and divine reason are imparted to your _____.

26. Faith gives you ears to hear what you cannot hear in the _____.

27. What types of things should you begin to expect hearing by the Spirit?

    _____

    _____

    _____

    _____

    _____

HAVING EYES TO SEE

28. Faith is never _____.

29. Faith sees the _____, not the problem. Faith sees the _____, not the question. Faith sees the _____, not the mess.

30. Too often, we don't watch with eyes of faith and, as a result, we miss the _____ right in front of us. Faith gives you eyes to see what God is _____ and where He is _____.

LEARNING TO SPEAK THE LANGUAGE OF FAITH

31. In the same way that faith hears and sees, it also has a _____.

32. Faith speaks about the promise as though already received, long before it is ever naturally _____, _____, or _____.

33. We _____ with our lips what we believe in our _____.

FLAVORS OF FAITH

34. Faith not only hears, sees and speaks. It also presses in to _____ the goodness of God.

35. The Scriptures tell us that God's Word is sweet like _____.

FAITH REQUIRES ACTION

36. The faith of God moves you to _____.

37. How has God's Spirit led you by faith in the past? And what were the results?

     _____

     _____

     _____

     _____

     _____

38. Everything about this faith realm is contingent upon our _____ to _____.

FAITH RECEIVES

39. Faith receives _____.

40. When God releases revelation, grab hold of it, even if your mind can't understand it, even if you can't seem to _____ it naturally.

41. Pull on the heavens. Pull by _____ and receive by _____.

FAITH REFUSES

42. Faith has the _____ and _____ to refuse.

43. Faith has the right to _____ sickness and disease.

44. What are some other things that faith can refuse?

_____

_____

_____

_____

_____

HOW THE FAITH REALM WORKS

45. According to Galatians 5:6, in its simplest terms, how does faith work?

_____

_____

46. Where there is great _____, there are always great _____.

47. Without love, faith is _____.

SHIFTING GEARS FROM REALM TO REALM

48. Faith is the _____ _____ for what God wants to unfold in our lives. It connects us to a fresh anointing that destroys barriers to God's blessing.

49. We must have faith in _____ through Jesus Christ (see Romans 10:9-10).

50. We must have faith in the _____ of God's Word (see 2 Timothy 3:15-17).

51. We must have faith in the _____ power of God's Spirit (see 1 Peter 1:3-5).

52. Faith _____ the realm of the superabundant anointing.

KEYS FOR ACTIVATION

ACTIVATION #1:

We've spoken about the spiritual senses that God wants to make come alive in your life through faith. Right now, I want you to offer your body, by faith, to the Spirit. Ask God to harmonize the spiritual and natural realms for you. Read Romans 6:13 and then begin to pray through the following chart:

DEDICATE	ACTIVATE
Eyes	See *by faith*
Ears	Hear *by faith*
Mouth	Taste *by faith*
Nose	Smell *by faith*
Hands	Touch *by faith*
Feet	Walk *by faith*

You can begin to move and perceive in the Spirit, even in the natural realm. This is the dimension where faith becomes a living reality. As you pray through this chart, you may even begin to receive tangible healing miracles for your physical body as God's faith begins to flow through you.

ACTIVATION #2:

Think of areas in which your faith seems to be weak. Then study particular parts of the Word of God that relate to that subject and begin proclaiming that Word over your life and all that pertains to you. In this way, let the faith of God enter your heart and mind to such a degree that it begins to control your words and actions.

Pay closer attention to your words in the coming days. Are you speaking words of faith or words of doubt? Start saying what God says, not what other people say.

Are you expecting an answer to your prayers? You should. God has promised:

If you believe, you will receive whatever you ask for in prayer. (Matthew 21:22)

Did He really say, *"whatever you ask"*? Yes, He did, and that promise is for you today. Don't let anything or anyone discourage you, for you are a child of the King and part of a chosen people, a royal priesthood, a holy nation. (See 1 Peter 2:9.) Through your faith in Christ, you *"can do all things"* (Philippians 4:13 NKJV).

REALMS OF ANOINTING

1. *"He has sent me to proclaim _____ for the prisoners and _____ _____ _____ for the blind, to set the oppressed free, to proclaim the year of the Lord's favor"* (Luke 4:18–19).

2. The anointing is the _____ _____ of God that sets us apart.

3. The anointing is the _____ to go, the _____ to do, the _____ to be, and the _____ to continue.

THE POWER OF ANOINTING

4. The anointing allows the gifts of the Spirit to _____ _____.

5. *"The Spirit of the LORD will come powerfully upon you, and you will prophesy with them; and you will be changed into a _____ _____"* (1 Samuel 10:6).

THE THREE DIMENSIONS OF THE ANOINTING

6.   In the same way that there are three realms in the Spirit (and in the last lesson I showed you the three dimensions of faith), you will see that there are also _____ _____ when it comes to the anointing.

7.   In biblical times, the anointing prepared the priests, prophets and kings to take up their position and (this is key) to _____ _____ _____.

8.   These specific anointings—_____, _____, _____ _____—are still available to us.

9.   What does this mean to you?

   _____

   _____

   _____

   _____

   _____

10. Without the anointing, _____ _____ could never develop properly, so the Spirit anoints ordinary believers because the task at hand is much _____ than the senior leaders of the church can accomplish on their own.

11. For every _____, there is a special _____.

12   Write down the three distinct expressions of the anointing within the Scriptures: _____ _____ _____, _____ _____ _____, _____ _____ ____.

THE OUTPOURING

13   When we pray and ask for a breakthrough, we must take time to listen to the instructions the Lord gives us. This is a _____ for operating in the _____. God will ask you to do something _____ so He can do something _____.

14.   The anointing that rests _____ you is able to work supernatural miracles _____ you.

THE COVERING

15.   As the Spirit smears His anointing over us, He covers us with a _____ _____ against the attacks of the enemy that try to bring irritation, frustration, sickness, or even death.

16.   Being covered by His anointing gives us _____ over obstacles and the ability to _____ any problem that presents itself.

17.   As we are anointed, we become the _____ of Christ in the earth.

THE MARINATING

18.   When this level of anointing is _____ into you, your _____ becomes _____.

19.   That _____ must die in order for your _____ to fly.

20.   The first two dimensions deal with the anointing _____ us, but this third dimension deals with the anointing _____ us.

21.   You can't get to the place in the glory that God wants to take you unless you _____ _____ in the anointing that He's given you.

22. The anointing comes ____ ____ __ _____, and one of its assignments is marinating you in God's _____ ____ _____.

23. At times, the process of the anointing may require _____ _____ of time and effort on our part in order to see the fullest effect.

GIVING THE ANOINTING AWAY

24. _____ _____ what God has blessed you with, so it can be a blessing to others. In this way, you position yourself to enter into __ _____ _____.

25. His anointing brings _____.

THE TRANSITION FROM ANOINTING TO GLORY

26. We use the realms of _____ and the realm of the _____ to bring us into the realms of _____.

27. Why would God enable and then disable us?

    _____

    _____

    _____

    _____

    _____

28. You may think of this transition in terms of a shuttle launch from _____ _____ to _____ around the universe. The anointing gives us God's power to be lifted into new realms of discovering Him in His glory.

KEYS FOR ACTIVATION

ACTIVATION #1.

Since we know that there is a special anointing for each special calling, consider this: have you moved into the anointing that corresponds to your calling? If not, it is available to you. Believe God for it today.

Since the anointing is activated by obedience to God's commands, is there something He has told you that you have been either afraid or unwilling to do? Concentrate on what God is saying to you privately and make a conscious effort to crucify the flesh that is preventing you from obeying. With obedience will come the change you need.

If your anointing has not been developing as it should, it might be because of an inconsistent prayer life, the fact that you are not giving out what God is blessing you with, or a simple lack of faith on your part. Position yourself to enter into a continual flow.

"God did extraordinary miracles through Paul, so that even handkerchiefs and aprons that had touched him were taken to the sick, and their illnesses were cured and the evil spirits left them." (Acts 19:11–12)

The God of Paul is ready to anoint you today for His glory.

ACTIVATION #2.

In Exodus 30:22–25, the Lord gives Moses a supernatural recipe for preparing the sacred anointing oil. It is a holy and fragrant blend. I have a friend who has received oil recipes on an occasional basis from an angel who comes to visit her. Even in our own ministry, there have been times when God has spoken to us specifically about preparing anointing oils for healing, deliverance, or other specific needs, all of which He blesses in a supernatural way.

Maybe the Spirit will lead you to prepare a sacred anointing oil. Several years ago, my friend Chris Harvey, while reflecting on his life, wrote a fun "personal recipe" for anointing oil. I want to share it with you:

The Anointing Oil Recipe

2 cups of brokenness	3 cups of weakness
4 cups of rejection	2 cups of betrayal
3 cups of misunderstanding	1 lb. of freshly ground frustration
1 packet of loneliness	3 packets of patience
2 bitter thorns for spice	a generous amount of hard times
5 gallons of tears	2 dozen spiritual songs
3 lbs. of sweet times	5 cups of grace
4 lbs. of intimacy butter	2 handfuls of wisdom sprinkles
3 cups of the essence of worship	4 packets of victory
1 good friend	1 dozen laughs

Put in the oven of life for twenty years, seven times hotter than average. Let cool for three years. Then share it with others, but sparingly, because it's rich stuff!

Can you relate to that recipe? God takes the bad times and mixes them with His goodness, and through it all, He pours His Spirit out upon us, covering us and marinating us in His anointing. What is the recipe for your personal anointing? Have fun writing it out here:

REALMS OF GLORY

1. Faith says God is _____, the anointing says God _____, but the glory says, "__ ____."

2. The glory is not limited by _____, _____ or _____. Neither is it limited by the _____ of man or earthly _____.

3. God is the _____, and the glory is _____.

4. Describe in your own words Isaiah's vision of the glory (Isaiah 6:2–4).

   _____

   _____

   _____

   _____

   _____

INVITE THE GLORY CLOUD

5. Describe in your own words Daniel's vision of the glory (Daniel 7:9–10).

   _____

   _____

   _____

   _____

   _____

6. What did John see? (Revelation 1:10–17).

   _____

   _____

   _____

   _____

7. The Spirit _____ to us today to _____ up, to _____ into the very presence of the Lord.

THE SPIRIT'S INVITATION

8. Be set _____ from any remaining _____. Deliverance comes with ease in the glory.

9. Know that in this glory realm there are _____ _____. In this realm, _____ is too difficult for God.

10. Your part is to _____ yourself as never before.

THE IDENTITY OF THE GLORY

11. Whereas the _____ defines the power of God, the _____ defines the person of God.

12. When we consider the trifold nature of God's identity, revealed through the Father, Son, and Holy Spirit, we behold the greater revelation of this _____.

13. According to Ephesians 1:17, God is the _____ of Glory.

14. According to Psalm 24:7, Jesus is the _____ of Glory.

15. According to 1 Peter 4:14, the Holy Spirit is the _____ of Glory.

SHINE IN THE GLORY

16. God's glory is realized even greater in the midst of _____. It causes us to _____ and _____.

17. The glory releases heaven's _____ upon our _____ and causes our spirits to _____.

THE THREE DIMENSIONS OF GLORY

18. Name the three dimensions of God's glory:

_____

_____

_____

19. Explain in your own words, what the *Doxa* Glory reveals:

_____

_____

_____

_____

_____

20. We must never think that we've seen _____ there is to see in God. So much _____ exists for those who choose to live in this _____ realm.

21. Explain in your own words, what the *Shekinah* Glory reveals:

_____

_____

_____

_____

_____

22. When this glory comes, it appears upon the young and the old, the saved and the unsaved. It is a sign of the glory, not of man, a sign that God desires to release His glory upon the

_____.

23. Explain in your own words, what the *Kabod* Glory reveals:

_____

_____

_____

_____

24. Instead of feeling the _____ of the world, we feel the _____ of the glory of God.

OPEN DOORS IN THE GLORY

25. The glory opens _____ that cannot be shut. It is, even now, opening doors _____ _____.

26. When you walk in the _____, you have nothing to fear. You no longer have to worry about doors being opened for you. Your gates will always stand _____.

27. When we _____ on the glory, we begin to place our trust in the answer.

THE SPONTANEITY OF THE GLORY

28. Following the leading of God's glory often teaches us to be _____.

29. In any situation, find what brings forth the _____ glory, and do _____ of it.

HOW THE GLORY REALM OPERATES

30. As we work in the _____, God works in the _____.

31. When the _____ comes, we stand in the _____ and allow God to do His work.

32. All that is required is _____ to the glory realm.

ASKING FOR NATIONS IN THE GLORY

33. The glory _____ your _____ and _____ your _____.

34. If we want to see God's purposes accelerated in the earth, we must become _____ _____

_____ _____.

35. Where do you feel a personal urgency to ask God for His glory? And what will you begin to do, to release it?

_____

_____

_____

BIRTHING GOD'S PURPOSES IN THE GLORY

36. In order to make a spiritual impact on a territorial, regional, or national level, it is imperative that you learn how to _____ _____ in the _____.

37. It will be the glory that makes the _____.

38. Those willing to _____ it and _____ in it will be _____ the farthest in this next move of the Spirit.

THE CLOUD OF GLORY

39. I have seen the cloud of God's glory roll into the sanctuary of churches. It often presents as a _____ or _____, but usually comes in slowly, much as a natural cloud drifts. We've even seen a _____ appear in the midst of the glory cloud.

40. Have you seen God's glory appear as a cloud, rainbow or other visible manifestation? If so, write down your encounter:

_____

_____

_____

41. Are these manifestations of glory clouds biblical? If so, where can they be found in Scripture? And what is the message that they bring?

_____

_____

_____

_____

WHEN THE GLORY COMES

42. The influence of God's glory _____ deep and wide. There is no place or person the glory cannot _____. There is no situation where the glory cannot _____ its miracle touch.

43. The glory is the realm of _____ power.

KEYS FOR ACTIVATION

ACTIVATION #1:

We've spoken about the many ways in which the Spirit has chosen to reveal His glory to saints in former times. How much more does the Spirit desire to reveal His glory to you today, now that you are in Christ. I want you to take some time and prepare yourself to encounter the Lord in His glory. You may want to set the atmosphere with a soaking worship CD. (I would recommend my *SpiritSpa* or *SpiritSpa 2* albums. They are available for purchase or digital download online). Get comfortable and in a position to see the Spirit reveal Himself to you. Close your eyes and ask God to give you a picture of His glory.

After your encounter, draw what you see.

You may not be an artist, and that's okay. Have fun with this activation and simply write down the words and sounds you heard. Draw the pictures and colors you saw. This personal picture will become a reminder to you of where God wants to take you. This drawing may even be prophetic in nature and reveal something to you about your spiritual gifts or where God is leading you in your future.

ACTIVATION #2.

In this lesson, you've learned that, at times, God's manifest glory has appeared as a weighty cloud of His presence. This is the *kabod* glory of God. This glory can be tangibly felt. By faith, ask God to reveal His *kabod* to you. Sense the anointing of God coming upon you as a heavenly oil, covering you for entrance into His glory. With your eyes closed (so that you can focus on these spiritual realities), begin lifting your hands into the glory. Reach into the glory and recognize the "weightiness" of this realm.

You may begin to feel a gentle weight upon your forehead or your shoulders. Some people have experienced a large hand-like pressure on their chest or back. This is the hand of God—the glory of His presence—touching you in a powerful way. Receive the impartations that come in the cloud of His glory. With uplifted hands, you may begin to notice a light and gentle pressure on your palms or forearms. Receive the gifts that are being given to you in this *kabod*.

ACTIVATION #3.

Another manifestation of God's glory is His visible *shekinah* realm. In this dimension of glory, the invisible realm becomes apparent in the natural, although it is not always recognized immediately without a quickening by the Spirit of God. Some of the manifestations that take place in this dimension are a golden glory revealed through the pores of your skin or resting upon your clothing or other objects such as a Bible, wallet, purse, or chair. Sometimes, this golden manifestation is so fine that it almost appears to look like "diamond dust." It can come in various colors, shapes, and forms, each bringing a specific message directly from God. We have seen this unique manifestation come upon people as silver, ruby, sapphire, emerald, and other colors of precious stones.

Lift your hands into the glory now and ask God to reveal His *shekinah* glory to you. Spend time worshiping the Lord in the beauty of His holiness. Once you sense the glory of God coming upon you, take a look at your hands, arms, or face, in a mirror if necessary. You may notice this *shekinah* glory beginning to appear. If you don't see it at first, don't become discouraged. Instead, posture yourself to embrace what God is doing and remain open for Him to reveal it to you in His timing. The times and moments when the *shekinah* glory begins to appear may surprise you and even bring a "spirit-answer" to some of your troubling questions.

PART II

MOVING IN THE SUPERNATURAL

REALMS OF DIVINE ASCENSION

1. What were the songs of ascents spoken of in Psalms (see page 89)?

   _____

   _____

   _____

   _____

2. Ruth Ward Heflin received a magnificent instruction from God: "Praise until the spirit of _____ comes. Worship until the _____ comes. Then _____ in the glory."

3. There's a difference between _____, _____, and the _____. We need to learn about and understand the difference between them.

4. We _____ from praise into _____ into _____ _____.

5. We _____ from _____ into _____ into _____

    _____.

6. We _____ from _____ _____ into the _____ _____ into the

    _____ __ _____.

7. We move from _____ to _____ to _____. These are the three
   realms that concern us. All the parts work together to create a heavenly wheel that accommodates
   the presence of the Living God.

OPENING THE DOOR FOR ENCOUNTER

8. The longest book in the Bible, the Psalms, is actually _____ _____.

9. Singing is the _____ of the heart, and therefore also the _____ of the
   spirit. Praise and worship position us ____ _____ Spirit to spirit.

10. When you do something you've _____ _____, you get results you've _____
    _____.

11. Whenever _____ _____ show up, _____ _____ always show up too.

12. With every _____ _____, there's a _____ _____, and with every _____ _____,
    there's a _____ _____.

MUSIC AND HEALING

13. Music is able to break down _____, open our _____, and soften our
    _____. It also creates an atmosphere conducive for _____.

14. As we touch the glory of God's _____ through our song, our body resonates in tune
    with the heavens. Our vibrational frequency ____ _____ with Jesus Christ.

15. What is the difference between a diseased cell and a normal cell? How can the right kind of music help the body come back into proper harmony?

_____

_____

_____

_____

_____

THE SONG IN YOU

16. Scientists have discovered that your DNA contains a _____ orchestral _____.

17. _____ are a _____!

18. In order for our bodies to be in _____ _____, we must come into alignment with the glory. Therefore, the Spirit's song must become _____ _____.

GOLD RECORDS FROM HEAVEN

19. The Spirit wants to upgrade your _____ and replace all of your old records with new _____ _____ from heaven.

20. God wants to give you _____ _____ and _____ _____ that will bring _____ _____.

21. Great _____ will come as God begins giving you His _____ _____.

SINGING THE NEW SONG

22. This requires a tolerance for _____ and a desire for _____.

23. When we sing the new song, our spirit _____ _____ to connect with the Spirit of God, to know His _____, His _____, His _____ and His _____.

24. What are the three keys for opening yourself to singing the new song?

    1). _____ _____ ____ _____ _____,

    2). _____ ____ _____ _____,

    3). _____ _____ _____ _____.

25. When you _____ the sound God places in your heart, it will open up an entirely new realm into the _____.

THE HIGH PRAISES OF GOD

26. God looks for us to give Him a _____ praise. The high praise can only come from the high _____! So, we must ascend.

27. What does it mean for *"the high praises of God to be in their mouth, and a two-edged sword in their hand"*?

    _____

    _____

    _____

PRAISE CHANGES THE ATMOSPHERE

28. Praise is a verb, an _____ _____, and every time we set out to praise the Lord, _____ should be involved.

29. I like telling people that I'm not praising because of what I'm going _____, but because of where I'm going _____. This puts us in _____ to move farther up the mountain of the Lord.

30. _____ praise brings forth _____ worship, which leads us into _____ glory. This is the _____ glory.

31. What does it mean when someone says "praise changes the atmosphere"? And is there any biblical evidence of this happening in Scripture?

_____

_____

_____

_____

_____

WORSHIP CARRIES US FURTHER

32. Worship is _____ God for who He is. Worship is _____ from praise. In worship, we move from a place of acknowledging God's acts and what He has done or what He is going to do, into a place of recognizing _____ _____ _____ and honoring Him.

33. Worship carries us into God's _____. It's the connection between the _____ realm and the _____ realm.

34. In the glory, there is a _____.

HOW THE REALMS OF PRAISE AND WORSHIP WORK TOGETHER

35. When we move into the glory through our _____ and _____, miracles happen automatically, without much effort on our part. We simply see what God is doing in _____, and honor His presence in _____. He responds to us in _____.

36. Fill out this chart to show how praise and worship work together to bring forth the glory:

In Praise	In Worship	In Glory

STANDING IN THE GLORY

37. Once you experience the cloud, all things are possible in that realm and that dimension—the _____ _____.

38. The ultimate goal of our praise and worship is _____ _____ to the glory realm of God.

39. This is an important foundation upon which you need to operate, not to see occasional signs and wonders in your life, but to live continuously in a _____ of the _____.

40. Only in the glory are we eternally _____. Only by the power of His glory can we experience the difference, a divine _____ in our life, and _____ begin to flow.

KEYS FOR ACTIVATION

ACTIVATION #1.

Determine to put into personal practice the three keys that you've learned for singing the new song. Go through each step every morning and find your new song for each day. This will set the tone for your day, your week, and your month, and enable you to discover new realms of God's glory. As a reminder, these are the three steps you must take:

1. **Make Music in Your Heart.** In other words, find the tune, melody, or chord pattern. Begin whistling it, humming it, or connecting with it in your own personal way. Just be sure to release the sound!

2. **Sing in the Spirit.** Now that you've found your song, begin singing over the melody with spiritual tongues. As you sing, it will be the Spirit of God singing through you. In this process, He is releasing His voice over the music. He is singing His song through you.

3. **Sing with Your Understanding.** After you've sung in the spirit, some known words or thoughts may begin to emerge (this usually happens within your mind). This is the Spirit of God bringing His revelation concerning the words He's been singing through you. Don't be afraid to step out in faith at this point and begin singing these words aloud. Sing what you're hearing. Sing what you're

feeling. Sing the new song that God is giving you. Allow this song to reach your innermost feelings and begin to respond to it. Don't worry about it being perfect. You may stumble over a few words. That's okay. God is giving you something new.

Enter into the joy of receiving this special gift from heaven. Connect to the revelation and receive it with gladness.

ACTIVATION #2.

In a corporate praise and worship setting, you may have the opportunity to invite others to ascend the mountain of the Lord with you. You don't need to be a worship leader to do this; you only need to be a willing participant with the Spirit of God! Be discerning of what God is doing in the atmosphere and join with others in joyful celebration. Let God use you to cultivate a corporate expression of praise. Some examples of this may be:

- Create "Glory Wheels" – This is when willing worshipers join their hands together, face inward, and dance together in a circle. The more participants there are, the larger the circle can be. Sometimes there might even be a wheel within a wheel!

- Start a "Glory Train" – This is when one person will invite others to join behind them in marching around the room. With enough participants, the marching line resembles a train heading into the glory!

- Invite others into a "Praise Wave" – You can easily do this with at least three participants who are willing to hold hands together, side by side, in a straight line, moving forward and backward (in the motion of a wave), inviting the waves of God's glory to wash over you as you give Him praise. At times, we have had entire congregations (hundreds of people) doing this all at once. It is a powerful demonstration of God's people praising Him in unity. See what Psalm 133 says about this.

As you corporately participate in praise and worship during church and conference meetings, begin to watch for the miracles. Become aware of changes in your physical body—the healing miracles that God is working inside of you! Also become aware of the change in the corporate atmosphere. Begin looking for signs and wonders all around you because they often manifest through the power of praise and worship!

ACTIVATION #3:

Take a SpiritSpa and soak with worship music! The Bible says that *"times of refreshing…come from the presence of the Lord"* (Acts 3:19 NKJV). Spend time in the atmosphere of God's presence by taking a daily (or weekly) SpiritSpa. You might wonder how to do this. It's easy! Just follow these simple instructions.

Turn on some peaceful worship music and lie down in a comfortable location. It is more ideal to listen to praise and worship through a sound system with speakers as opposed to headphones, as the cells of your physical body will "listen" and begin to positively respond to the anointed music. Remember, praise and worship has the ability to bring not just spiritual and emotional healing but also increased healing on a physical level. When the music stops, bask in the silence and begin to listen for the still small voice of the Lord.

I would recommend using one of my soaking albums for your SpiritSpa session. The following albums are highly recommended: *SpiritSpa, SpiritSpa 2, Receive Your Healing,* and *Experience His Glory.* All of these albums have instrumental tracks without words for your listening pleasure.

REALMS OF ANGELIC PRESENCE

1. *"There is _____ in the presence of the angels of God"* (Luke 15:10).

2. Where there is _____, there are _____, and where there are _____, there is _____. You can't separate them.

SPIRITUAL GUARDIANS

3. Angels are assigned as spiritual _____ and _____ over your life, and many scriptures confirm this.

4. Guardian angels look like the _____ to whom they are _____.

5. What scriptural proof do we have for the existence of guardian angels?

_____

_____

_____

_____

OTHER IMPORTANT TRUTHS ABOUT THE ANGELIC REALM

6. Angels are mentioned at least _____ times in the Old Testament and _____ times in the New Testament.

7. What does the word *angel* mean? _____

8. Angels are intricately involved in the work of God on the earth. They _____ the life of the believer.

9. Every individual is _____ at least one angel from birth. (See Psalm 91:11.)

10. Name at least three other important truths about the angelic realm:

_____

_____

_____

THE NATURE OF ANGELS

11. Name at least three things about the nature of angels:

_____

_____

_____

THE NAMES OF ANGELS

12. Give at least three of the names the Bible gives to angels:

     _____

     _____

     _____

13. What was the name of Manoah's angel? _____

THE THREE-FOLD PURPOSE OF ANGELS

14. What is the three-fold purpose of angels?

     1. _____

     2. _____

     3. _____

THE ANGELS OF THE NATIONS

15. Not only are angels available to assist us in our _____ lives, but God has also created angels that interact in the affairs of _____.

EVEN JESUS NEEDED THE MINISTRY OF ANGELS

16. While Jesus prayed in the garden of Gethsemane, God sent an _____ to help Him.

17. The Bible makes it clear that Jesus received _____ through the ministry of an _____.

ANGELS BRING US JOY

18. What is the purpose of the holy laughter that angels bring?

_____

_____

_____

ANGELS DELIVER MIRACLES AND REVELATION

19. Angels don't do the miracles. They _____ them. They're not originating the revelation; they're _____ the revelation.

20. God uses angelic ministry in the same way that we use _____.

ACTIVATING THE ANGELS: THE SIT PRINCIPLE

21. What do I mean by the SIT Principle?

S _____

I _____

T _____

22. Under the old covenant, the people of God didn't have authority to _____ _____. Today angels wait for us to command them, because we have been given _____ over them in the name of Jesus.

23. The Scriptures say that we will _____ angels. You cannot _____ something unless you have _____ _____ over it.

24. When you enter into the flow of _____ into the heavens, purposing in your heart to

_____ in the way God desires, the way the Scriptures teach, your generosity rises before God as

a _____, and heaven takes notice.

KEYS FOR ACTIVATION

ACTIVATION #1.

Become more familiar with your surroundings. Begin to pay attention to things like flashes of light, unexplainable sounds, unusual or sudden appearances of rainbows, light breezes, or other small changes in the atmospheric conditions around you. These could be the presence of God's ministering angels reaching out to connect with you. When you begin to notice these signs, prayerfully consult the Lord and ask Him what He is doing and revealing to you. He is able to bring you personal guidance and revelation through these encounters.

ACTIVATION #2.

Take notice of your photographs. Many people are beginning to notice the angelic realm appearing in their digital photography as "heavenly lights." Learn to discern the difference between moisture or dust particles and genuine supernatural orbs appearing in your photos. When you see these orbs, or other super-natural images, ask the Lord what He is saying to you through it.

Many years ago, the Spirit revealed to me that images of orbs are the "gifts" or "anointings" that are being delivered to God's people through the ministry of angels. So when we see an orb, it is not an actual angel, but, instead, the gift that angel is carrying to God's servant. Take notice of the color, shape, or other details, as it all contains a prophetic message that needs to be understood.

ACTIVATION #3.

Read and meditate on God's Word. You can use the time before bed to meditate on God's Word and read biblical accounts of angelic visitation. My book, *Seeing Angels*, has an appendix of 394 Scripture verses about angels, providing some amazing biblical testimonies! At night, you are the most relaxed and, therefore, God is able to use this time to speak to you and show you the angelic realm through dreams and visions. Another highly recommended book that I wrote is called *Encountering Your Angels*, which includes fifty-two reflections on the ministry of angels in the Bible and how they apply to your own life.

REALMS OF THE MIRACULOUS

1. How does the dictionary define the word *miracle?*

    _____

    _____

    _____

2. A miracle is something only _____ can do.

3. The _____ thing is that He wants to release His _____ through _____
    and _____.

MIRACLE FOUNDATIONS IN FAITH

4. What are the three qualifications for operating in creative miracles?

    1. _____

2. _____

3. _____

FAITH FOR HEALING

5. What three steps to receive salvation are the same as the steps required to receive physical healing?

   1. _____

   2. _____

   3. _____

6. How do we pull the invisible into the visible plane?

   _____

   _____

   _____

   _____

GREAT LOVE PRODUCES GREAT MIRACLES

7. Great miracles happen when we develop compassion for the sick and hurting because God's _____ flows through us.

WORKING MIRACLES IN THE ANOINTING

8. The way God releases His _____ through you varies according to the situation and the specific instruction you receive from heaven. This requires your _____ to flow in obedience with the anointing.

SUPERNATURAL METHODS FOR WORKING MIRACLES

9. Various styles and techniques are used when _____ _____.

10. There are many different methods of laying hands on the sick. Let the _____ lead you.

11. Don't be afraid of coming into contact with sickness. If you're filled with the Holy Spirit, you are anointed to _____ _____. Every sickness must yield to the power of healing that flows through you.

12. When you reach out to heal the sick, your hands become the _____ for heaven to touch earth. Embrace that truth as you begin working miracles.

DEMONSTRATION BRINGS MANIFESTATION

13. Give at least three examples of working unusual miracles from the Bible.

    1. _____

    2. _____

    3. _____

MOVING INTO MIRACLE-WORKING GLORY

14. When God's miracles are shared, _____ is released in that testimony, opening a realm for somebody else to experience the same dimension of God's goodness.

15. Looking for sickness and pain pulls you back into the realm of _____ _____.

RELEASING ANGELIC MINISTERS IN THE GLORY

16. As we minister in the glory cloud, _____ are an integral part of that
    _____.

17. Angels bring _____ _____ from the invisible into the
    visible realms.

18. In the Scriptures, angels are referred to as _____ _____.

19. Angels must be _____ in order to be _____.

SIGNS AND WONDERS IN THE GLORY

20. We do not command signs and wonders to come forth as much as we _____ for them to
    appear and _____ the movement of God within the glory realm.

21. Define the word *sign:*

    _____

    _____

    _____

    _____

THE VOICE OF THE SIGN

22. Signs convey a specific _____ while the Spirit speaks in the language of
    _____.

23. To _____ His signs is to _____ His voice. If we _____ His signs, we
    _____ His voice.

24. A holy sign from God always points you to the _____ and _____ of _____ _____.

RECOGNIZING THE SIGNS

25. Signs _____ our _____.

26. They must be _____.

27. As we fix our eyes on the _____ realm, we see the signs that God gives us. The signs, however, are not the _____. The _____ _____ _____ is always our main focus.

THE DIFFERENCE BETWEEN SIGNS AND WONDERS

28. Define the word *wonder:*

_____

_____

_____

29. God's wonders are _____, and He receives all the glory.

WHAT SHOULD WE EXPECT?

30. Name at least three of the signs and wonders we should all expect in our lives and ministries:

1. _____

2. _____

3. _____

KEYS FOR ACTIVATION

ACTIVATION #1

Begin to learn how to harness the "electricity of the Spirit." In the same way that the power of electricity is not realized unless a connection is made, you must make a connection in the Spirit to bring forth the power of signs and wonders. Here are the steps:

1. Understand that the gospel is the power of God! According to Romans 1:16–17, when we share the gospel message, it is the righteousness of God revealed from faith to faith. Our boldly spoken declaration of God's Word makes the initial connection.

2. Recognize that the power of the gospel must be seen! God does not want to hide the evidence of His Word from people. Quite to the contrary: He desires to demonstrate it for all to see. Paul said, "*My speech and my preaching was* not with enticing words of man's wisdom, but in demonstration of the Spirit and of power" (1 Corinthians 2:4 KJV). Begin to recognize the current of God's power that is being released as you speak His Word. Sometimes the power will be released as healing miracles. At other times, it may be a financial breakthrough, depending on what part of God's Word you put a demand on. Signs and wonders will be seen when you speak God's Word, but they must be recognized.

3. Know that the power of the gospel will be demonstrated through you! God will use you to reveal the miracle to others. Once you have spoken the Word, and you recognize the power of God beginning to flow, don't be afraid to step fully into it by working miracles. Boldly speak the instructions of God to those who are present or within your current situation. Step out in miraculous faith and let the signs and wonders be seen in you! (See Acts 1:8.)

ACTIVATION #2

Here are some simple steps for ministering healing to the sick.

1. Find out what the problem or medical condition is. Sometimes the Lord may reveal this to you by a word of knowledge; if He does, don't be afraid to step out in faith and share what you've received. At other times, however, you may need to ask the person you're ministering to about their pain, ailment or disease. This will help you to focus both the spoken word and your healing method on the specific area of need.

2. Share a healing promise from God's Word with the person you're ministering to. Ask them to come into agreement with that Word, because God's Word always works.

3. Decide which biblical healing method to use and then do it! There are many methods found within the Scriptures, for example:

   o Lay your hands on the sick. (See Matthew 18:19; Mark 16:18, 1:40–42, 5:35–40, 7:32–35.) Make sure you ask for permission before using this method. Also, be sensitive and use wisdom and discretion when praying in this way.

   o Ask the sick to lay their hands on you. (See Mark 6:56, 5:25–34; Luke 6:19.) Ask the person in need to hold your hand, touch your shoulder, or make a physical connection in some other way. Again, be sensitive and use wisdom and discretion. This can be a powerful method for healing, especially when you feel a strong anointing flowing through you.

   o Anoint the sick with oil. (See Mark 6:12–13; James 5:14–15.)

   o Use a point of contact to release the miracle. (See Acts 19:11–12.) This method for healing can be especially helpful when ministering to someone from a distance. When using this method, simply pray over an object (a handkerchief, towel, or piece of cloth) and allow the Lord to anoint it for His healing power to be delivered. Ask a person who is present (a family member or friend) to take the anointed object to the person who needs a healing breakthrough. We have successfully used this method of healing many times when ministering to those who are sick in the hospital or even unsaved loved ones who are not present.

4. Ask the recipient to do something they weren't able to do before. (See Mark 2:10–12, 3:5, 8:23–25.) This is asking them to put their faith into action. As they step out in bold faith, encourage them to look for the healing miracle! We see this scriptural response in the Bible helping many people to connect with their miracle:

    o   The blind man put his faith into action by washing in the pool. (See John 9:1–7.)

    o   The withered hand was stretched forth in obedience to Jesus's command. (See Luke 6:6–10.)

    o   The leper dipped in the water seven times and was made whole. (See 2 Kings 5:1–14.)

PART III

MOVING IN THE HEAVENLIES

REALMS OF MANIFESTING WEALTH

1. *"And my God will meet all your needs according to the riches of* _____ _____ *in Christ Jesus"* (Philippians 4:19).

2. The glory holds many _____.

THE THREE DIMENSIONS OF MANIFESTING WEALTH

3. What are the three dimensions of manifesting wealth?

   1. _____

   2. _____

   3. _____

BLESSING: THE COVENANT CONNECTOR

4. God's _____ are mentioned more than six hundred times in the Scriptures.

5. When we speak about _____ in the area of _____, we begin by addressing the issue of _____.

6. Abraham _____ to King Melchizedek four hundred years before the old covenant was ever put into place. (See Genesis 14:20; Hebrews 7:12.)

7. We don't tithe to _____ a _____.

8. We tithe to break _____ with the _____ of _____ over our finances.

9. _____ of _____ and uncertainties about the future have prevented some from being generous. This must change if we truly want to connect to the _____ dimension.

FAVOR: DIVINE ASSIGNMENT AND DIVINE ALIGNMENT

10. The connection between our _____ and _____ works in the same way as the connection between the _____ and _____.

11. Information is useless without a _____. Information can cause you to know about favor and yet still lack results. But a revelation will cause you to move toward an _____ in order to produce a manifestation of the impartation.

12. King David delighted to see his people _____ _____ to the Lord (see 1 Chronicles 29:9).

13. How is an offering different from the tithe?

_____

_____

_____

_____

14. How does faith come?

_____

_____

_____

_____

15. How do we present an offering to God in faith?

_____

_____

_____

_____

INCREASE: THE POWER OF THE SEED

16. The Spirit gives us the _____ to either sow the seed or keep it. But we receive increase in this dimension according to the seed sown, depending on what we have _____ in our heart to do.

17. Define the word *sow*.

_____

_____

18. The farthest distance between you and your harvest is simply your seed. Your seed moves you closer to _____ _____.

19. The Spirit releases His _____ into the midst of our _____.

DIVINE TRANSFERENCE OF WEALTH

20. Just as Isaiah prophesied, the Spirit wants to give you: "_____ _____, *riches stored in secret places, so that you may know that I am the* L*ord*" (Isaiah 45:3).

21. Miracles happen quickly in the glory because it is the realm of _____. When you sow into the glory realm, you reap from that realm of _____ _____.

22. As the glory changes you, it also changes your _____.

KEYS FOR ACTIVATION

ACTIVATION #1:

This entire lesson is a practical activation that you can begin applying to your life immediately. If you haven't participated in tithes, offerings, or sowing seed in the past, don't become discouraged. Instead, choose to participate with this new revelation that you've now received. Once you begin putting these principles into action, you should begin keeping a record of what you've given and the harvests you've received. This is a fun way to see the practicality of these teachings. Some of the blessings that you will begin to receive might be small, while others will come in large sizes. Don't dismiss any of them. Instead, rejoice in all the blessing, favor, and increase the Spirit begins to bring to you. As you begin to recognize this abundance, it will cause you to continue in this lifestyle of supernatural generosity!

ACTIVATION #2:

Take a small step toward generosity today by giving something meaningful to someone else. You might want to bless someone with a cup of coffee at the coffee shop today. Or you could give away a special article of clothing to someone you know. Watch how God uses this simple action to bring blessings, not only to the receiver but also back to you as the generous giver.

ACTIVATION #3:

Today, make a list of five reasons you're blessed. Use this list in your prayers this week, thanking the Lord for His goodness and His blessings that fill your life. Watch and see how your thankfulness begins to change the atmosphere and helps to open your eyes to see even more blessing around you. At the end of the week, step out and bless someone else in an extraordinary way.

REALMS OF SPIRIT TRAVEL

1. When we speak about moving in the glory, we must also consider the supernatural ways in which the glory _____ _____!

2. What are the two biblical ways that God can supernaturally move us in the Spirit?

   1. Divine _____

   2. Divine _____

3. If you are out of your body, then it's a _____ experience.

4. If you are in your body, then it's _____ by the Spirit.

5. When you are _____ in the Spirit, God can move your spirit into _____, _____ or even _____ _____.

WALK, RUN, SOAR!

6. *"But they that wait upon the* Lord *shall renew their strength; they shall mount up with wings as eagles; they shall _____, and not be weary; and they shall _____, and not faint"* (Isaiah 40:31 kjv).

7. It's easy to become tired from doing the same old thing. That's why the Spirit has opened up this further dimension, so we can _____ _____ in the glory.

FINDING YOUR SPIRIT WINGS

8. God has given you _____.

9. We are _____ human beings to whom God has given the means to _____.

CARRIED AWAY IN THE SPIRIT

10. As Ezekiel looked upon these angelic cherubim, he noticed many things, but what drew his attention most was _____ _____.

11. Ezekiel went from seeing the living creatures and noticing the _____ and _____ of their wings, to having their wings come upon him.

SEEING GOD'S WILL

12. During his encounter, Ezekiel was called on to _____ to the dry bones.

13. As you travel in the Spirit, expect there to be times when God calls on you to _____. In that moment, you will be made to understand the will of God, and you can then _____ it.

HOW TO DISCERN THE REALM

14.   We discern what something is by the _____ it produces.

15.   What questions are helpful when it comes to discerning these realms?

      1. _____

      2. _____

      3. _____

NIGHT ENCOUNTERS

16.   Why do many translation experiences occur at night?

      _____

      _____

      _____

17.   As the sons and daughters of God, we must be willing to be led at all times in all locations. Let us become _____ _____ to the guidance and direction of the Spirit.

TRANSLATED IN THE CANADIAN ARCTIC

18.   Paul said, *"In the body or out of the body I do not know"* (2 Corinthians 12:2). He wasn't sure if he was _____ or not, but knew he had been caught up to the _____ _____.

19.   God said to me, "My abundance comes as my Spirit and truth is _____ and _____."

TRANSPORTED BY THE SPIRIT

20. In a mere second, like a flash, you can move to another location on the planet, bypassing all

_____ _____.

21. Define the Greek word *harpazo:*

_____

_____

_____

CARS, BOATS, AND OTHER OBJECTS TRANSPORTED

22. Not only can the Spirit supernaturally move people, but it can also move _____,

finances, missing items—the possibilities are _____!

WALKING THROUGH WALLS AND WALKING INTO HEAVEN

23. What supernatural thing did Jesus do in John 20:19?

_____

_____

_____

24. What revelatory message did Jesus give His disciples?

_____

_____

_____

_____

25. If Jesus was _____, and He is our _____, we should _____ for this _____ too.

KEYS FOR ACTIVATION

ACTIVATION:

If you desire to be used by God in this very supernatural way, you can begin posturing yourself for these experiences. It is common for people to begin experiencing being "translated by the Spirit" in the middle of the night, while they are sleeping. Sometimes what you may initially think was a dream could actually have been a real-life scenario that you were engaging with by means of your spirit-man. Here are some very practical ways you can begin positioning yourself for such an encounter:

#1. Before bedtime, spend time in the Word, reading the Scriptures and asking the Spirit to make them come alive for you. In addition to your daily devotional reading, find some scriptural passages that speak about the unusual prophetic encounters of Isaiah, Ezekiel, John the Revelator, or others. Believe that God desires to give you unusual prophetic encounters as well.

#2. When you first shut your eyes to go to sleep, ask the Spirit to play the Scriptures back to you as a movie in your mind. Allow Him to take you *into* the Scriptures, to *see* them come alive!

REALMS OF HEAVENLY ENCOUNTER

1. We travel through this earthly life with a mandate from God to _____ the lost, _____ the sick, and bring _____ to the captives.

2. Our real home is a _____ one. That's why we carry such a desire within us to go deeper in the things of God.

3. What does Hebrews 11:14–16 mean to you?

   _____

   _____

   _____

   _____

4. Today, as children of a better covenant, we see heaven coming to earth in response to the prayers of Jesus. Our longing for this heavenly homeland creates a suction in the Spirit that pulls those things that are _____ into the realm of _____ _____.

THE THREE REALMS OF HEAVEN

5. What are the three realms of heaven?

    1. _____

    2. _____

    3. _____

6. Describe each of these three realms of heaven in your own words:

    1. _____

    2. _____

    3. _____

7. We need to be careful how much we share with others about our _____ _____. Some things the Spirit shares with you are for your own spiritual journey and should not be shared with others.

YOUR PRAYERS AND THE REALMS OF HEAVEN

8. When Jesus was on the earth, He taught His disciples how to pray, using a very specific model. What is that model, found in Matthew 6:9–10?

    _____

    _____

    _____

    _____

9. Heaven, for most people, is a mysterious place far away, but we have the opportunity to make it an integral part of our _____ _____.

HEAVEN COMING TO EARTH

10. What images do you see in your mind when you think about heaven coming to earth? Explain:

   _____

   _____

   _____

   _____

   _____

11. Whatever you focus on increases in your life. True or false? T _____ F _____

12. Recently, more people are experiencing the _____ of heaven.

FEASTING IN HEAVEN

13. Describe some impartations that are available in the realms of heavenly glory:

   _____

   _____

   _____

   _____

   _____

14. Don't be afraid to receive what the Spirit gives to you in _____ _____.

THE ETERNAL REALM

15.   What does *eternal life* mean?

_____

_____

A BELIEVER NEVER DIES

16.   My body isn't who I am. It's just my _____. I am a spirit, and my spirit will never _____.

17.   According to the Scriptures, the bodies of departed saints have been transformed into bodies that _____ _____.

THE SAINTLY DEPARTED

18.   Many people on earth right now may be completely oblivious of heaven, and maybe you have been this way in the past, but I can tell you this: the people in heaven, the saints of God there, are _____ _____ to what is happening here on the earth.

19.   We are _____ by the great cloud of witnesses, as the saints watch from their perspective in heavenly glory. These saints, patriarchs and ancients have been surrounding us and are watching, beholding, and _____ _____ ____.

A GREAT CLOUD OF WITNESSES

20.   In ancient Greece, what were the highest bleachers called? _____

21.   What does the phrase *compassed about* mean?

_____

_____

22. The saints of old are able to bring us _____ and _____ and even

_____, but this is orchestrated by God, and not something that we should try to pursue

on our own merit.

MESSAGES FROM THE REALM BEYOND

23. We never worship the things that come from heaven. Instead, we worship the _____ who is the

light of heaven! We worship _____ _____—Him and Him alone.

SEEK FIRST HIS KINGDOM

24. In the glory, we are not permitted to _____ with the dead, and we do not

_____ them.

25. God has a living cloud of witnesses that surrounds our lives continuously, a cloud of saints who

are alive and well in the heavenly realm. Our God is not the God of the _____, but of the

_____.

GLORIOUS ENCOUNTERS IN THE REALM OF THE LIVING

26. We don't worship the saints of the past. We don't worship the ones who have gone on before. We

worship _____.

WHAT HAPPENS TO THE DEAD?

27. When a person has died and gone to hell, and later seems to be appearing to the living, this is a

_____ spirit, or what Scriptures call a "_____ spirit." That is *not* a God

encounter.

TEST THE SPIRITS

28. We do not call on any other name except the name of _____. When we call on His name, He will visit us in His glory in new and unusual ways.

GREATER GLORY

29. One encounter with glory changes _____. In the Spirit, new things are birthed, new callings, giftings, and anointings come to us, and the Spirit prepares us to be a _____ to the _____ , to be utilized in a miraculous way.

FOUND IN CHRIST

30. When we are found in _____ , we will not experience _____.

RESTORED TO LIVE AGAIN

31. When Jesus Christ came to the earth as the last Adam, He _____ _____ with and _____ humanity to an intimate relationship with God.

32. As Jesus hung on the cross of Calvary, He took upon Himself all of the _____ for our wrongdoing.

33. Many people strive and struggle and don't understand that God did not intend for them to live in a constant _____ ____ _____ . His intention was that we labor to enter into the _____ ____ _____ _____ .

DEATH HAS BEEN DEFEATED

34. When Jesus rose from the dead, I was there with Him, being raised up into a new place of life, into a new place of _____ _____ , into a new place of living.

35. I love the atmosphere of glory. As you step into it, the reality of God _____ _____ .

KEYS FOR ACTIVATION

ACTIVATION #1:

You must have an expectation for invitation. If you read Revelation 4:1–2, you will discover that John the Revelator was given an invitation from the Lord. The invitation was: *"Come up here,"* and the Spirit invited John through the open door. A good place to begin would be by meditating upon the Word of God. In Psalm 16:8, King David said, *"I have set the LORD continually before me; because He is at my right hand, I will not be shaken"* (AMP). This is how we can begin sitting at His feet. Focus on the following Scriptures and allow the glory of the Word to consume you:

- Psalm 46:10
- Psalm 99:5
- Psalm 132:7
- Matthew 5:35
- James 4:8

When we spend time in the presence of the Lord, we must become still before Him, so that we can hear His invitation and see the heavenly door being opened for us. After you read the Word, give yourself time to embrace it. Remember, it is important to respond to the realm. God will give us an invitation, and then we have a window of opportunity to respond. Don't hesitate. Don't delay. When God speaks, respond and walk through the open door of encounter.

ACTIVATION #2:

You can worship your way into the heavenlies (for help in praise and worship, read chapter 4 and follow the practical keys provided). Every time you begin praising and worshiping the Lord, whether in a private setting or in a corporate gathering, purpose in your heart to praise and worship until you find yourself in the heavens. Remember, heaven is simply the complete revelation of who God is. He is perfect. He is whole. He is good. Once you are in the heavens, begin to take notice of what God is speaking to you or revealing to you. Make sure to journal your experiences so that you can later reflect on them and watch them increase and expand.

ACTIVATION #3

Because heaven is a realm where creativity flows with ease, begin asking the Spirit for heavenly downloads. He wants to give you new ideas, witty inventions, supernatural creations, accurate skills, profound wisdom, etc., so begin to ask for it. As you spend more time in the heavens, you will be more effective here on the earth.

STUDY GUIDE ANSWER KEY

LESSON 1: REALMS OF FAITH

1. "God has dealt to every man the measure of faith."

2. God-faith

3. Stretched

4. Give your own answer

5. Faith

6. It is small but spicy; it is the greatest among all the garden plants; it is substantial enough to provide shade and safety.

7. Purpose

8. Spiritual experiences

9. Substance; evidence

10. Foundation

11. Listen to the voice of God's spirit; read and study God's everlasting word; speak God's Word with authority and boldness.

12. Discovery; faith

13. The belief; trust in; loyalty; firm belief

14. Now; not yet; promises

15. Delivers

16. Future

17. Mindsets

18. Something stale; something fresh

19. Evidence

20. 1). Little faith, the faith we all have;
    2). Great faith, a faith that believes in God, trusts His word and His power, and presents itself to him to receive (by faith) what it needs; and
    3). Perfect faith, the faith of God.

21. Great faith

22. In; of; now

23. Crucified; faith

24. The universal, divine reason or mind of God

25. Word by faith; spirit

26. Natural

27. Give your own answer

28. Blind

29. Solution; answer; miracle

30. Miracle; doing; leading

31. Voice

32. Felt; seen; heard

33. Confess; spirit

34. Taste

35. Honey

36. Action

37. Give your own answer

38. Willingness; respond

39. Now

40. Graspe

41. Faith; faith

42. Ability; right

43. Refuse

44. Give your own answers

45. By love

46. Love; miracles

47. Broken

48. Beginning point

49. Salvation

50. Authority

51. Supernatural

52. Activates

LESSON 2: REALMS OF ANOINTING

1. Freedom; recovery of sight

2. Manifest power

3. Favor; grace; power; strength

4. Function freely

5. Different person

6. Three dimensions

7. Do their job

8. Priestly, prophetic, and kingly

9. Give your own answer

10. Your calling; greater

11. Call; anointing

12. To pour out, to smear over, to rub in

13. Key; anointing; possible; impossible

14. Upon; for

15. Supernatural protection

16. Power; overcome

17. Fragrance

18. Rubbed; flesh; uncomfortable

19. Flesh; spirit

20. Upon; within

21. Push through

22. To do a job; process of preparation

23. Greater sacrifices

24. Give away; a continual flow

25. Breakthrough

26. Faith; anointing; glory

27. The anointing enables us, and we swim in the river of God. The glory disables us, because when it comes, we surf on the waves of the spirit's flow.

28. Blast off; orbiting

LESSON 3: REALMS OF GLORY

1. Present; rewards; I am

2. Time; space; circumstance; mind; ability

3. Glory; God

4. Give your own answer

5. Give your own answer

6. Give your own answer

7. Calls; come; ascend

8. Free; shackles

9. No impossibilities; nothing

10. Open

11. Anointing; glory

12. Glory

13. Father

14. King

15. Spirit

16. Darkness; arise; shine

17. Radiance; countenance; shine

18. The Doxa glory; the Shekinah glory; the Kabod glory

19. Give your own answer

20. All; more; glory

21. Give your own answer

22. Nations

23. Give your own answer

24. Weight; weight

25. Doors; for you

26. Glory; open

27. Focus

28. Spontaneous

29. Most; more

30. Anointing; glory

31. Glory; glory

32. Yielding

33. Multiplies; impact; increases; witness

34. People of the glory

35. Give your own answer

36. Birth things; glory

37. Difference

38. Receive; flow; carried

39. Haze; smoke; rainbow

40. Give your own answer

41. Give your own answer

42. Spreads; reach; extend

43. Highest

PART II: MOVING IN THE SUPERNATURAL

LESSON 4: REALMS OF DIVINE ASCENSION

1. Many scholars believe that these Psalms were sung by Hebrew worshipers as they ascended the road to Zion to attend the three major feasts: Passover, Pentecost, and Tabernacles.

2. Worship; glory; stand

3. Praise; worship; glory

4. Move; worship; manifest glory

5. Move; shouting; talking; intimate whispering

6. Move; outer court; holy place; holy of holies

7. Faith; anointing; glory

8. God's songbook

9. Language; language; to connect

10. Never done; never had

11. New songs; new blessings

12. New day; new song; new song; new glory

13. Barriers; minds; hearts; miracles

14. Presence; is realigned

15. Give your own answers (hint: the answers are found on page 92 of the book, *Moving in Glory Realms.*)

16. Beautiful; score

17. You; song

18. Perfect harmony; our song

19. Sound; gold records

20. New sounds; new songs; new successes

21. Joy; new sounds

22. Change; more

23. Reaches out; heart; will; intention; words

24. 1). Make music in your heart;

    2). Sing in the Spirit;

    3). Sing with your understanding.

25. Release; supernatural

26. High; place

27. Give your own answer. (Hint: the answer is found on page 99 of *Moving in Glory Realms*.)

28. Action word; action

29. Through; to; motion

30. Corporate; corporate; corporate; greater

31. Give your own answer

32. Acknowledging; different; who he is

33. Heart; praise; glory

34. Knowing

35. Praise; worship; praise; worship; glory

36. Give your own answer (if you need help, see page 104 of *Moving in Glory Realms*)

37. Glory realm

38. Complete surrender

39. Dimension; miraculous

40. Changed; shift; miracles

LESSON 5: REALMS OF ANGELIC PRESENCE

1. Rejoicing

2. Glory; angels; angels; glory

3. Guardians; protectors

4. Person; assigned

5. Psalm 91:11-12; Matthew 18:10; Hebrews 1:14; Revelation 8:3-4

6. 108; 165

7. Messenger or sent one

8. Encircle

9. Assigned

10. (Possible answers) Angels are never to be worshiped; angels are immortal and have great strength but are not omnipotent; angels do not need to rest or sleep; angels are commonly seen in large numbers; angels are not glorified human beings; most angelic beings do not have wings; some angels can't be trusted

11. (Possible answers) Angels do not have permanent physical bodies; angels are capable of traveling very fast; angels can only be in one place at a time; angels receive assignments and dedicate themselves to those assignments; angels can take on the appearance of either men or women; they can also manifest in various sizes and physical forms, including animal likenesses

12. (Possible answers) Watchers; God's host; Holy ones; The Sons of God; Three men

13. Wonderful

14. To acclaim God; to act in spiritual combat; to otherwise assist mankind

15. Personal; countries

16. Angel

17. Strength; angel

18. It brings supernatural strength to those who are suffering from depression or those who have experienced terrible abuse or trauma.

19. Deliver; delivering

20. Fedex

21. **S**peak the word; **I**ntercede (spend time in prayer); **T**ouch God through your giving

22. Command angels; authority

23. Judge; judge; legal authority

24. Sowing; give; memorial

LESSON 6: REALMS OF THE MIRACULOUS

1. "An effect or extraordinary event in the physical world that surpasses all known human or natural powers and is ascribed to a supernatural cause."

2. God

3. Amazing; miracles; you; me

4. 1.) You must have faith for miracles;
   2.) You must be anointed with power;
   3.) You must yield to God and flow in his glory

5. 1.) You hear the Word of God;
   2.) You believe the Word in your heart;
   3.) You confess faith in Christ unto salvation (healing in this case)

6. Through faith, we put a demand on the supernatural and move it into our natural realm. Find what you need in the word, believe God's Word in your heart, and take action toward it.

7. Love

8. Healing; willingness

9. Working miracles

10. Spirit

11. Work miracles

12. Portals

13. (Possible answers)

    1.) Moses stretched forth his rod to part the Red Sea (see Exodus 14:16);

    2.) Elisha threw down his mantle to divide the waters of the Jordan river (see 2 Kings 2:14);

    3.) Paul said, *"My message and my preaching were not with wise and persuasive words, but with a demonstration of the Spirit's power"* (1 Corinthians 2:4);

    4.) Jesus made mud with his spit and put it into a blind man's eyes, and he recovered his sight (see John 9:6–7);

    5.) Jesus cast demons out of a man everybody thought was crazy, sending them into a herd of pigs, and delivered him (see Luke 8:26–33);

    6.) Jesus pulled money out of a fish's mouth in order to pay his taxes (see Matthew 17:24–27)

14. Victory

15. Natural limitation

16. Angels; interaction

17. Supernatural substances

18. Spirit winds

19. Recognized; utilized

20. Watch; recognize

21. "A token; indication; any object, action, event, pattern, etc. That conveys a meaning; a conventional or arbitrary mark figure, or symbol used as an abbreviation for the word or the words it represents; a notice, bearing a name, direction, warning, or advertisement that is displayed or posted for public view."

22. Message; miracles

23. Ignore; ignore 2x (conversely, to hear his signs is to hear his voice)

24. Person; presence; Jesus Christ

25. Follow; lives

26. Noticed

27. Glory; focus; glory of God

28. "Something strange and surprising; a cause of surprise, astonishment, or admiration; a miraculous deed or event, a remarkable phenomenon."

29. Marvelous

30. (Possible answers) casting out demons, speaking in new tongues, healing the sick (see Mark 16:17–18); raising the dead and cleansing those who are diseased (see Matthew 10:8); holy laughter (see Proverbs 17:22, Psalm 2:4, 126:2 and Job 8:21); being drunk on new wine (see Acts 2:15 and 2 Corinthians 5:13); trembling and vibrating in the spirit (see Exodus 19:16, Daniel 10:10, Isaiah 6:4 and Acts 4:31); falling under the power of God (see Ezekiel 1:28, Matthew 17:6, Acts 9:4 and Revelation 1:17); being caught up in trances and visions (see Acts 10:10 and 22:17); remaining speechless and filled with awe (see Daniel 10:15 and Luke 1:22); experiencing extraordinary manifestations of golden glory (see Exodus 34:30).

PART III: MOVING IN THE HEAVENLIES

LESSON 7: REALMS OF MANIFESTING WEALTH

1. His glory

2. Riches

3. 1.) Blessing, the covenant connector;

   2.) Favor, divine assignment and divine alignment; and

   3.) Increase, the power of the seed

4. Blessings

5. Faith; finances; tithing

6. Tithed

7. Break; curse

8. Agreement, spirit; fear

9. Fear; lack; blessing

10. Offerings; favor; tithe; blessing

11. Revelation; activation

12. Give willingly

13. Give your own answer

14. Give your own answer

15. Give your own answer

16. Choice; purposed

17. "To plant seed for growth, especially by scattering; to set something in motion."

18. Your future

19. Possibilities; impossibilities

20. Hidden treasures

21. Eternity; unlimited potential

22. Outcomes

LESSON 8: REALMS OF SPIRIT TRAVEL

1. Moves us

2. Translation; transportation

3. Translation

4. Transportation

5. Translated; past; present; future events

6. Run; walk

7. Rise higher

8. Wings

9. Redeemed; fly

10. Their wings

11. Sound; movement

12. Prophesy

13. Prophesy; decree

14. Fruit

15. 1.) Is it contradictory to the scriptures?;
    2.) Does it lower Jesus Christ from the Godhead?;
    3.) Does it glorify God?

16. During the nighttime, we are in a totally relaxed state in our bodies.

17. More sensitive

18. Translated; third heaven

19. Revealed; accepted

20. Natural restraints

21. "To seize, catch away, pluck, pull or take away by force."

22. Objects; unlimited

23. He suddenly appeared inside a room that had been locked. In other words, he walked through walls.

24. *"Peace be with you! As the father has sent me, I am sending you"* (John 20:21).

25. Transported; example; trust; miracle

LESSON 9: REALMS OF HEAVENLY ENCOUNTER

1. Win; heal; deliverance

2. Heavenly

3. Give your own answer

4. Eternal; natural manifestation

5. 1.) The first Heaven;
   2.) The second Heaven;
   3.) The third Heaven

6. Check your answer with the book (pages 188–191)

7. Heavenly encounters

8. *"Our father which art in Heaven, hallowed be Thy name. Thy kingdom come. Thy will be done in earth, as it is in Heaven"* (Matthew 6:9–10 KJV).

9. Everyday life

10. Give your own answer

11. True

12. Reality

13. Give your own answer (if you need help, see pages 194 and 195 of *Moving in Glory Realms*.)

14. The glory

15. It simply means you will live forever

16. Earthsuit; die

17. Never die

18. Not oblivious

19. Surrounded; cheering us on

20. The clouds

21. "To be completely encircled by something that is piled high all around you on every single side."

22. Messages; gifts; mantels

23. One; Jesus Christ

24. Communicate; summon

25. Dead; living

26. Jesus

27. Demonic; familiar

28. Jesus

29. Everything; blessing; nations

30. Christ; death

31. Reconnected; restored

32. Curse

33. Cycle of struggles; place of His rest

34. Resurrection glory

35. Comes alive

ABOUT THE AUTHOR

Joshua Mills is an internationally recognized ordained minister of the gospel, as well as a recording artist, keynote conference speaker, and author of more than twenty books and spiritual training manuals. His recent books include *Moving in Glory Realms* and *Seeing Angels*. He is well known for his unique insights into the glory realm, prophetic sound, and the supernatural atmosphere that he carries. For more than twenty years, he has helped people discover the life-shifting truth of salvation, healing, and deliverance for spirit, soul and body. Joshua and his wife, Janet, cofounded International Glory Ministries, and have ministered on six continents in over seventy-five nations around the world. Featured in several film documentaries and print articles, including *Charisma* and *Worship Leader Magazine*, together, they have ministered to millions around the world through radio, television, and online webcasts, including appearances on TBN, Daystar, GodTV, *It's Supernatural! with Sid Roth, 100 Huntley Street,* and *Everlasting Love* with Patricia King. Their ministry is located in both Palm Springs, California, and London, Ontario, Canada, where they live with their three children: Lincoln, Liberty, and Legacy.

OTHER BOOKS BY JOSHUA MILLS:

Seeing Angels: How to Recognize and Interact with Your Heavenly Messengers

Seeing Angels Study Guide

Encountering Your Angels: Biblical Proof that Angels Are Here to Help

Encountering Your Angels Study Guide

Power Portals: Awaken Your Connection to the Spirit Realm (coming in October 2020)

Power Portals Study Guide (coming in October 2020)